MEDIUM HIGH

Songs of Peace and Patriotism
for Solo Singers

10 Contemporary Settings for Solo Voice and Piano
For Recitals, Concerts, and Contests

COMPOSED AND ARRANGED BY JAY ALTHOUSE

Table of Contents

Sally K. Albrecht, Piano • Kent Heckman, Engineer
Piano accompaniments were recorded at Red Rock Recording in Saylorsburg, PA.

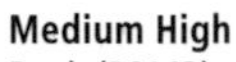

Medium High

Book (38143)	ISBN-10: 0-7390-8802-5	ISBN-13: 978-0-7390-8802-9
Accompaniment CD (38144)	ISBN-10: 0-7390-8803-3	ISBN-13: 978-0-7390-8803-6
Book & CD (38145)	ISBN-10: 0-7390-8804-1	ISBN-13: 978-0-7390-8804-3

Medium Low

Book (38146)	ISBN-10: 0-7390-8805-X	ISBN-13: 978-0-7390-8805-0
Accompaniment CD (38147)	ISBN-10: 0-7390-8806-8	ISBN-13: 978-0-7390-8806-7
Book & CD (38148)	ISBN-10: 0-7390-8807-6	ISBN-13: 978-0-7390-8807-4

Alfred Cares. Contents printed on 100% recycled paper.

1. AMAZING GRACE

Arranged by
JAY ALTHOUSE

Early American Melody
Words by **JOHN NEWTON**

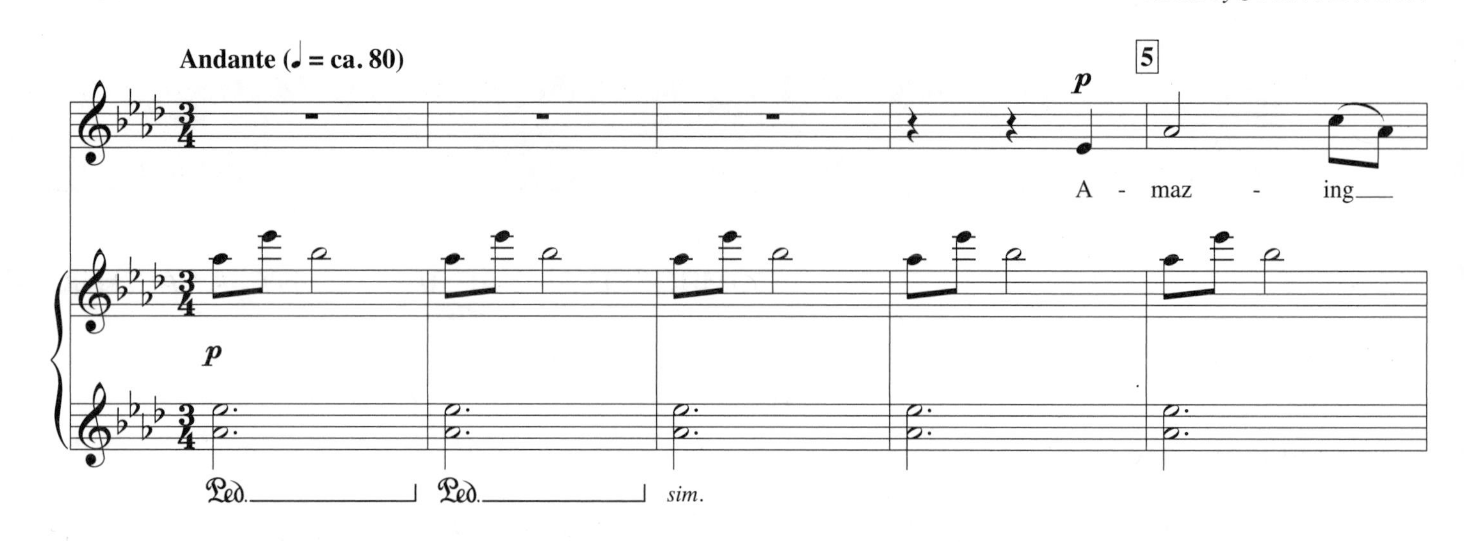

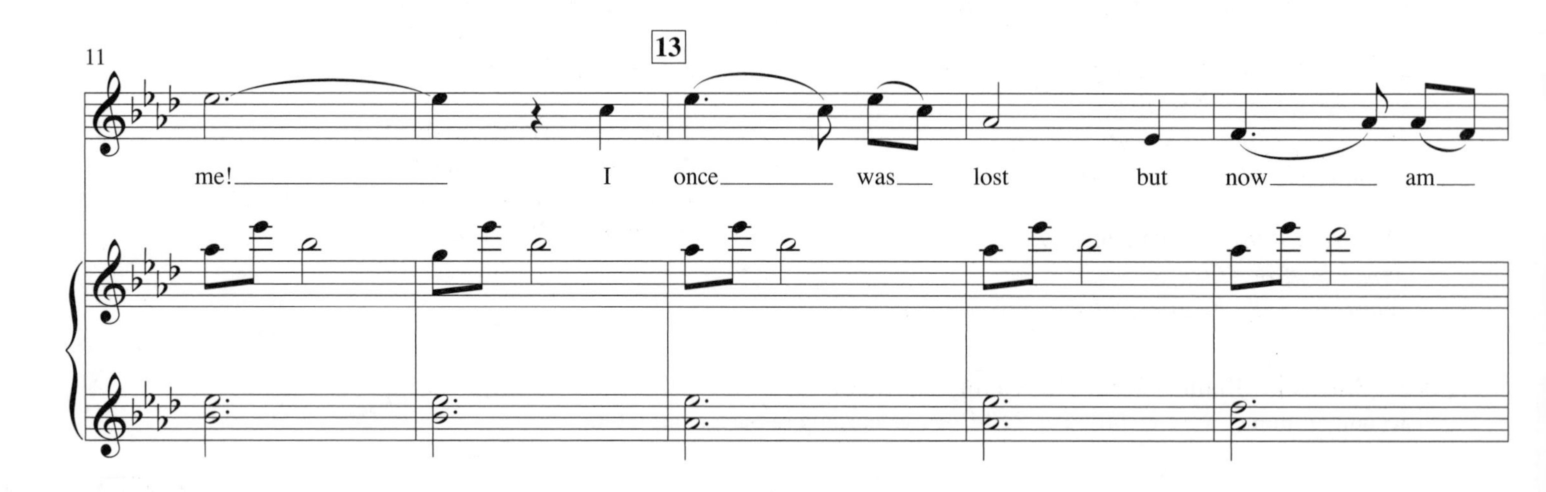

16
poco rit.
a tempo
found, was blind, but now I see.
poco rit.
mf a tempo
21
mf
23
Through man - y dan - gers, toils, and
26
snares, I have al - read - y come. 'Tis
31
grace hath brought me safe thus far, and grace will

36
lead me home.
8va
decresc.
41
rit.
mp
44
quasi-rubato
When we've been there ten
rit.
mp
quasi-rubato
46
cresc.
mf cresc.
thou - sand years, bright shin - ing as the sun,
cresc.
mf
cresc.
51
52
f
decresc.
we've no less days to sing God's praise than
f
decresc.

Tempo I
56
mp
when we've first be - gun.
mp
decresc.
61
p
62
rit.
A - maz - ing grace, how
p
rit.
66
sweet the sound.
Ped.

2. AMERICA, THE BEAUTIFUL

Arranged by
JAY ALTHOUSE

Music by **SAMUEL A. WARD**
Words by **KATHERINE LEE BATES**

13
rit.
shed His grace on thee, And crown thy good with broth - er-hood, from sea to shin - ing
rit.
18
With a bit more movement (♩ = ca. 80), gospel-style swing
20
sea. O, beau - ti - ful for
21
pa - triot dream that sees be - yond the years. Thine
24
al - a - bas - ter cit - ies gleam, un - dimmed by hu - man

27
28
tears. A - mer - i - ca! A - mer - i - ca! God
30
shed His grace on thee, And crown thy good with
33
broth - er - hood from sea to shin - ing sea. O,
36
beau - ti - ful for spa - cious skies, for am - ber waves of

39
grain, For pur - ple moun - tain maj - es-ties a -
42
44
bove the fruit - ed plain. A - mer - i - ca! A -
45
mer - i - ca! God shed His grace on thee, And
48
crown thy good with broth - er-hood from sea to shin - ing

51
52
ff
sea, from sea to shin - ing
ff
3
54
sea. A - mer - i - ca!
straight eighths

3. BATTLE HYMN OF THE REPUBLIC

Arranged by
JAY ALTHOUSE

Music by **WILLIAM STEFFE**
Words by **JULIA WARD HOWE**

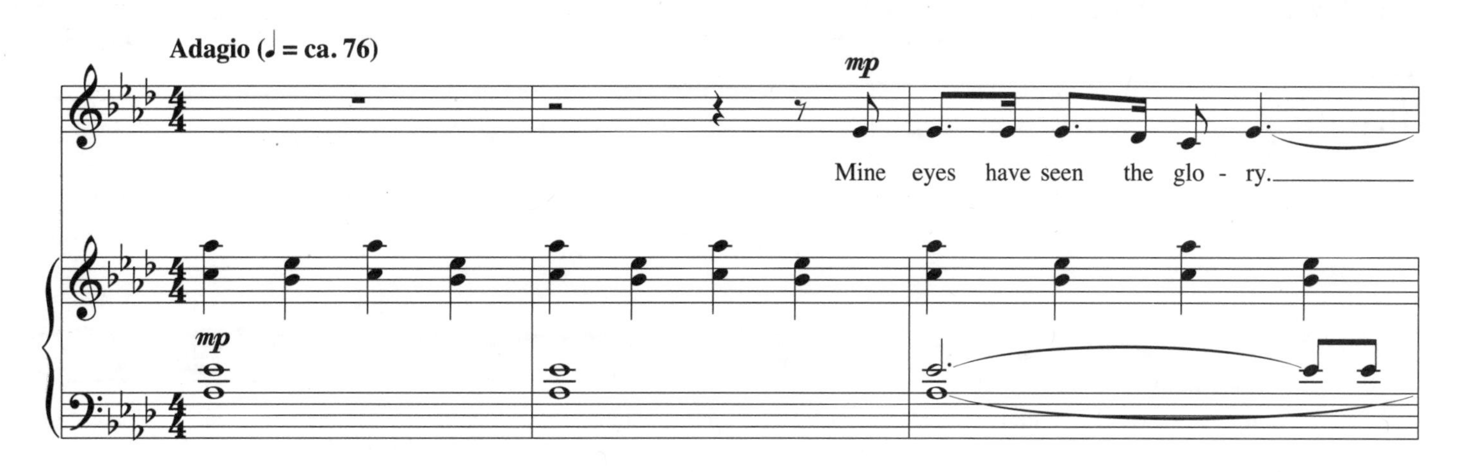

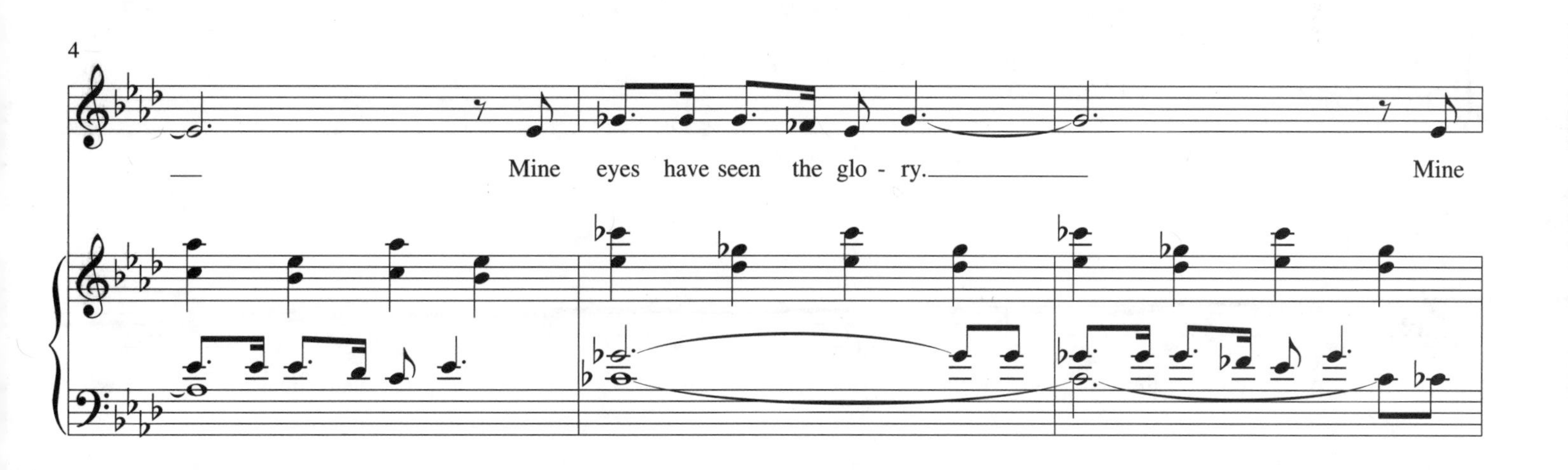

11
With a definite pulse (♩ = ca. 76)
on. Mine eyes have seen the glo - ry of the
14
com - ing of the Lord. He is tram - pling out the vin - tage where the
16
grapes of wrath are stored. He hath loosed the fate - ful light - ning of His
18
ter - ri-ble swift sword. His truth is march - ing on.

21
With a bit more movement (♩ = ca. 80)
mf
Glo - ry, glo - ry, hal - le - lu - jah! Glo - ry, glo - ry, hal - le -
mf
24
lu - jah! Glo - ry, glo - ry, hal - le - lu - jah! His
27
poco rit.
mp
truth is march - ing on. I have
decresc.
poco rit.
30
A bit slower, as before (♩ = ca. 76)
seen Him in the watch - fires of a hun - dred cir - cling camps. They have
mp

32
build - ed Him an al - tar in the eve - ning dews and damps. I can
34
read His right - eous sen - tence by the dim and flar - ing lamps. His
36
day is march - ing on.
38
With a bit more movement (♩ = ca. 80)
mf
Glo - ry, glo - ry, hal - le - lu - jah! Glo - ry, glo - ry, hal - le -
mf

41
lu - jah! Glo - ry, glo - ry, hal - le - lu - jah! His
44
slowing
truth is march - ing on.
slowing
decresc.
47
Slowly, freely, rubato
mp
In the beau - ty of the lil - ies Christ was born a - cross the
mp
51
sea, with a glo - ry in His bos - om that trans - fig - ures you and

55
56
me. As He died to make men ho - ly, let us
58
cresc.
live to make men free, while God is march - ing
cresc.
62
With a definite pulse (♩ = ca. 60)
mf
on.
mf cresc.
64
f
molto rit.
molto rit.

66
Spirited (♩ = ca. 84-88)
f
Glo - ry, glo - ry, hal - le - lu - jah! Glo - ry, glo - ry, hal - le -
8vb
69
rit.
lu - jah! Glo - ry, glo - ry, hal - le - lu - jah! His truth is march - ing
8vb
73
a tempo cresc. poco a poco
on, march-ing on. His truth is
76
rit. to end
fff
march - ing on!
rit. to end.

4. HOW CAN I KEEP FROM SINGING?

Arranged by
JAY ALTHOUSE

Quaker Song

14
all the tu - mult and the strife I hear the mu - sic ring-ing. It finds an ech - o
19
in my soul. How can I keep from sing-ing?
24
27
While though the tem - pest
28
loud - ly roars, I hear the truth: it liv - eth. And though the dark - ness

32
35
'round me close, songs in the night it giv - eth. No storm can shake my
36
in - most calm while to that rock I'm cling - ing. Since love is lord of
(Christ)
40
heav'n and earth, how can I keep from sing - ing?
8va
45
46
My life flows on in end - less song, a - bove earth's lam - en -

49
ta - tion. I hear the real though far off song that hails a new cre -
53
54
a - tion. Through all the tu - mult and the strife I hear the mu - sic
57
ring - ing. It finds an ech - o in my soul. How can I keep from
61
rit.
Slowly, freely
sing - ing? How can I keep from sing - ing?
rit.

A different version of this piece was performed by the San Francisco Girls' and Boys' Choirs at the inauguration of President Barack Obama, January 20, 2009

5. I HEAR AMERICA SINGING!
(An American Medley)

Arranged, with new Words and Music, by
SALLY K. ALBRECHT *and* **JAY ALTHOUSE**

13
SPOKEN: I like to see a man proud of the place in which he lives. I like to see a man live so that his place will be proud of him. - Abraham Lincoln
With energy (♩ = ca. 132)
decresc.
mf
17
SPOKEN: Where liberty dwells, there is my country. - Benjamin Franklin
21
mf
My coun - try 'tis of thee, sweet land of lib - er - ty,
25
of thee I sing.

28
SPOKEN: I only regret that I have but one life to lose for my country. - Nathan Hale
32
Land where my fa - thers died, land of the
35
Pil - grim's pride, from ev - 'ry moun - tain - side let
cresc.
cresc.
38
free - dom ring. 'Tis the
f
f
mf
decresc.

43
gift to be sim-ple, 'tis the gift to be free.
mf
47 SPOKEN: Freedom has its life in the hearts, the actions, the spirit of men. - Dwight D. Eisenhower
mf
'Tis the
51
gift to come down where we ought to be.
55 SPOKEN: We stand for freedom. That is our conviction for ourselves. That is our only commitment to others. - John F. Kennedy
mf
We are

59
grad. decresc.
free! We are free!
grad. decresc.
63
rit.
mp
65
Andante, with freedom of movement (♩ = ca. 88-92)
O, beau - ti - ful for
rit.
mp
66
spa - cious skies, for am - ber waves of grain, for pur - ple moun - tain
70
cresc.
rit.
f
maj - es - ties a - bove the fruit - ed plain! A -
cresc.
rit.
f

74
a tempo
mer - i - ca! A - mer - i - ca! God shed His grace on
a tempo
77
thee, and crown thy good with broth - er - hood from
80
decresc. e rit.
sea to shin - ing sea!
decresc. e rit.
84
Moderato (♩ = ca. 112)
SPOKEN: Give me your tired, your poor. Your huddled masses yearning to breathe free.
mp

89
The wretched refuse of your teeming shore. Send these, the homeless, tempest-tossed to me. I lift my lamp beside the golden door! - Emma Lazarus
93
96
mf
Let mu - sic
mf
97
swell the breeze, and ring from all the trees, sweet free - dom's
101
102
song. Let mor - tal tongues a - wake, let all that

105
cresc.
breathe par - take; let rocks their si - lence break,
cresc.
108
f rit.
110
With energy (♩ = ca. 112)
the sound pro - long.
f
rit.
112
I hear A - mer - i - ca sing - ing! I hear A - mer - i - ca sing - ing! A -
116
cresc. to end
molto rit.
ff
mer - i - ca, A - mer - i - ca, A - mer - i - ca!
cresc. to end
molto rit.
ff

6. OF THEE I SING, AMERICA!
(incorporating "America")

Music by **JAY ALTHOUSE**
Words by **SALLY K. ALBRECHT**
and **JAY ALTHOUSE**

13
14
mf
From snow-capped moun - tain rang - es
mf
16
to o-ceans white with foam. From the Col - o - ra - do plain to the
19
22
f
rock-y coast of Maine, this is the land we call home. Of thee I sing, A -
f
23
mer - i - ca. My coun-try 'tis of thee. Of thee I sing, A -

27
mer - i - ca, from sea to shin - ing sea.
31
A bit faster
mf
My coun - try 'tis of thee, sweet land of lib - er - ty,
mf
35
37
of thee I sing. Land where my fa - thers died,
39
land of the Pil - grim's pride, from ev - 'ry moun - tain-side let

43
cresc.
poco rit.
45
Tempo I
f
free - dom ring.
Of thee I sing, A - mer - i - ca.
cresc.
poco rit.
f
47
My coun-try 'tis of thee.
Of thee I sing, A - mer - i - ca,
51
53
from sea to shin - ing sea,
from sea to shin - ing sea,
56
rit.
ff
from sea to sea,
A - mer - i - ca!
rit.
ff
8va

7. PEACE LIKE A RIVER

Arranged by
JAY ALTHOUSE

American Folk Song

8
soul. I've got peace like a riv - er, I've got
10
peace like a riv - er, I've got peace like a riv - er in my
12
soul. I've got
15
love like an o-cean, I've got love like an o-cean, I've got love like an o-cean in my

18
soul. I've got love like an o-cean, I've got love like an o-cean, I've got
21
love like an o - cean in my soul. I've got
mf
mf
23
joy like a foun-tain, I've got joy like a foun-tain, I've got joy like a foun-tain in my
26
soul. I've got joy like a foun-tain, I've got joy like a foun-tain, I've got

29
joy like a foun-tain in my soul.
mp
32
mp
33
I've got peace like a riv - er, I've got peace like a riv - er, I've got
35
rit.
peace like a riv - er in my soul.
rit.

8. SIMPLE GIFTS

Arranged by
JAY ALTHOUSE

American Shaker Song
Attributed to JOSEPH BRACKET, JR.
Second verse by JAY ALTHOUSE

17
— 'twill be in the val - ley of love and de - light.
21
When true sim - plic - i - ty is gained, to bow and to bend we shan't be a - shamed. To
25
turn, turn, will be our de - light, till by turn - ing, turn - ing we
29
come 'round right. 'Tis the
mf

34
gift to be lov - ing, 'tis the gift to be kind. 'Tis the gift of grace we know that we will find. And
38
when we see the light at the break of day, we'll know that the truth will show us the way.
42
When true sim - plic - i - ty is gained, to bow and to bend we shan't be a - shamed. To
46
turn, turn, will be our de - light, till by turn - ing, turn - ing we

50
53
f
come 'round right. 'Tis the gift to be sim - ple, 'tis the
54
gift to be free. 'Tis the gift to come down where we ought to be. And
57
when we find our - selves in the place just right, 'twill be in the val - ley of love and de - light.
61
When true sim - plic - i - ty is gained, to bow and to bend we shan't be a - shamed. To

65
turn, turn, will be our de-light,
till by turn-ing, turn-ing we
69
come 'round right.
mf
73
mf
'Tis the gift,
rit.
mp
'tis the gift, 'tis the
rit.
77
Slowly, freely
p
gift to be sim-ple and free.
mp
p

9. SONG OF PEACE

Arranged by
JAY ALTHOUSE

Music by **FREDERIC CHOPIN***
Words by **JAY ALTHOUSE**

* From Etude in E Major, Op. 10, No. 3

10
rit.
11
mp a tempo
peace ev - er - more. Grant un - to us, o, grant us peace.
rit.
mp a tempo
13
O, grant us peace in time of trib - u - la - tion. O, grant us peace.
16
mf cresc. poco a poco
May our world be free of strife, and may we live a wor - thy life, and
mf cresc. poco a poco
18
f holding back
ff
in tempo decresc.
may our peace be ev - er - last - ing. Do - na no - bis pa - cem. Do - na no - bis
f holding back
ff
in tempo decresc.

21
p
pa - cem. Grant us peace for ev - er - more.
p decresc.
24
25
pp
Grant us peace
pp
27
rit.
ev - er - more. Peace.
rit.

10. THE STAR-SPANGLED BANNER
(in B-flat)

Arranged by
JAY ALTHOUSE

Music by **JOHN STAFFORD SMITH**
Words by **FRANCIS SCOTT KEY**

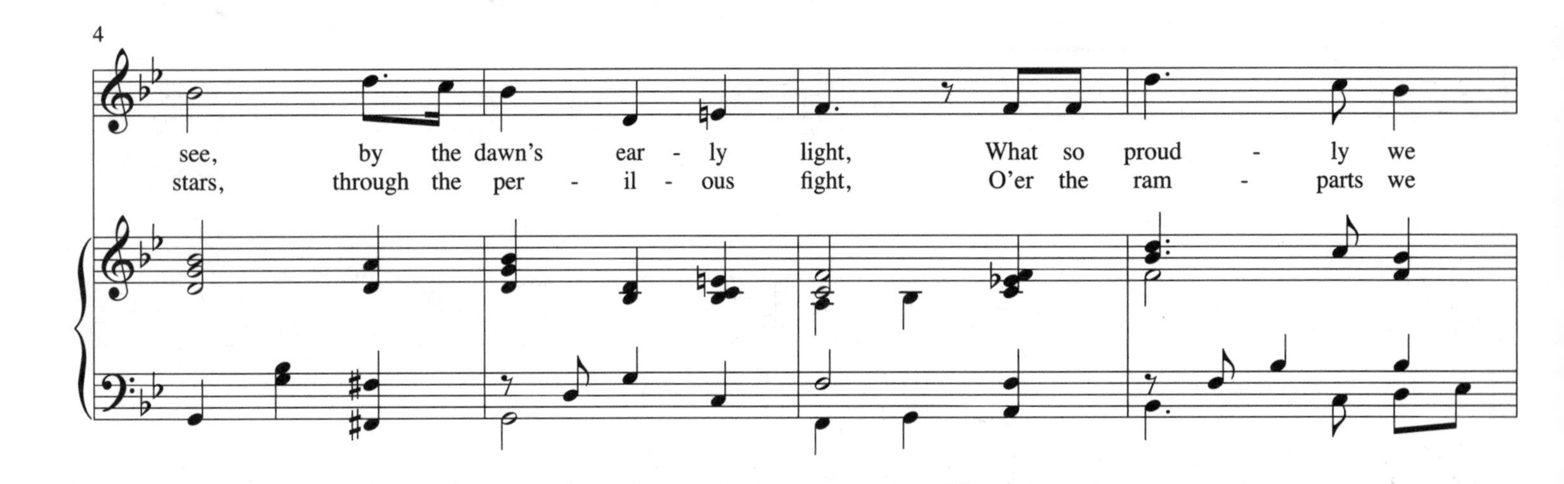

12
rock - ets' red glare, the bombs burst - ing in air, Gave
16
20
proof through the night that our flag was still there. O say, does that
21
cresc.
ff
rit.
star - span - gled ban - ner yet wave O'er the land of the
25
Freely
free and the home of the brave?

11. THE STAR-SPANGLED BANNER
(in C)

Arranged by
JAY ALTHOUSE

Music by **JOHN STAFFORD SMITH**
Words by **FRANCIS SCOTT KEY**

12
rock - ets' red glare, the bombs burst - ing in air, Gave
16
20
proof through the night that our flag was still there. O say, does that
21
cresc.
ff
rit.
star - span - gled ban - ner yet wave O'er the land of the
cresc.
ff
rit.
25
Freely
free and the home of the brave?

About the Composer/Arranger

JAY ALTHOUSE received a B.S. degree in Music Education and an M.Ed. degree in Music from Indiana University of Pennsylvania, from which he received the school's Distinguished Alumni award in 2004. For eight years he served as a rights and licenses administrator for a major educational music publisher. During that time he served a term on the Executive Board of the Music Publishers Association of America. For 20 years Jay was a choral editor for Alfred Music Publishing, but now he writes and arranges full time.

As a composer of choral music, Mr. Althouse has over 600 works in print for choirs of all levels. He is a writer member of ASCAP and is a regular recipient of the ASCAP Special Award for his compositions in the area of standard music. Jay has also co-written several songbooks, musicals, and cantatas with his wife, Sally K. Albrecht, and also compiled and arranged a number of highly regarded vocal solo collections, including *Folk Songs for Solo Singers, Volumes 1* and *2*. He is the co-writer of two best-selling Alfred books, *The Complete Choral Warm-Up Book* and *Accent on Composers*. Most recently, he completed three reproducible texts for the music classroom: *Ready to Read Music*, *60 Music Quizzes*, and *One-Page Composer Bios*. All are available from Alfred.

Sally and Jay have been happily married since 1985 and currently enjoy living in Raleigh, North Carolina, where Jay serves on the board of the North Carolina Master Chorale. Sally and Jay were honored to have their composition "I Hear America Singing!" performed during the 2009 Presidential Inauguration Ceremonies. In his spare time, Jay enjoys cooking (and eating).

Alfred Vocal Collections Arranged and/or Edited by Jay Althouse

- American Folk Songs for Solo Singers
- Christmas for Solo Singers
- Encores for Solo Singers
- Folk Songs for Solo Singers, Volumes 1 and 2
- Folk Songs for Two
- Great American Songwriters for Solo Singers
- International Folk Songs for Solo Singers
- Love Songs for Solo Singers
- Ready to Sing . . . Christmas
- Ready to Sing . . . Folk Songs
- Ready to Sing . . . Spirituals
- Sacred Solos for All Seasons
- Songs of Peace and Patriotism for Solo Singers
- Spirituals for Solo Singers, Volume 1
- Standards for Solo Singers
- Ye Shall Have a Song